What on Earth Is That?

World Book, Inc.
180 North LaSalle Street
Suite 900
Chicago, Illinois 60601
USA

For information about other World Book publications, visit our website at **www.worldbook.com** or call **1-800-WORLDBK (967-5325)**.

Library of Congress Cataloging-in-Publication data has been applied for.
Title: Ugh! Yuck! and Whoa! What on Earth Is That?
ISBN: 978-0-7166-3713-4

Ugh! Yuck! and Whoa!
ISBN: 978-0-7166-3708-0 (set, hc)

Also available as:
ISBN: 978-0-7166-3721-9 (e-book)

Introduction

Nature is filled with some amazing creatures. From ocean bottoms to mountain tops, from hot deserts to freezing tundra, the *Ugh! Yuck! and Whoa!* books highlight the most extreme animals: the grossest, the deadliest, the strangest, and the ugliest! This book is all about unusual animals you may never have heard of. Some live in the deep ocean, dense rain forests, or other places that people don't often go. Some are nocturnal, meaning they only come out at night. Some are very **rare,** meaning there aren't many of them around. There are so many species of amazing animals in all parts of the world. Scientists discover new animals all the time! There are still so many we have yet to find. Read on to learn about some of the coolest animals you've never seen before! Maybe someday you'll discover a new animal, too. This Strange Scale meter will show how unusual each animal is!

WOBBEGONG

Wobbegongs have huge mouths and sharp teeth. They have "beards" of growths that help wobbegongs blend in and attract **prey** to eat.

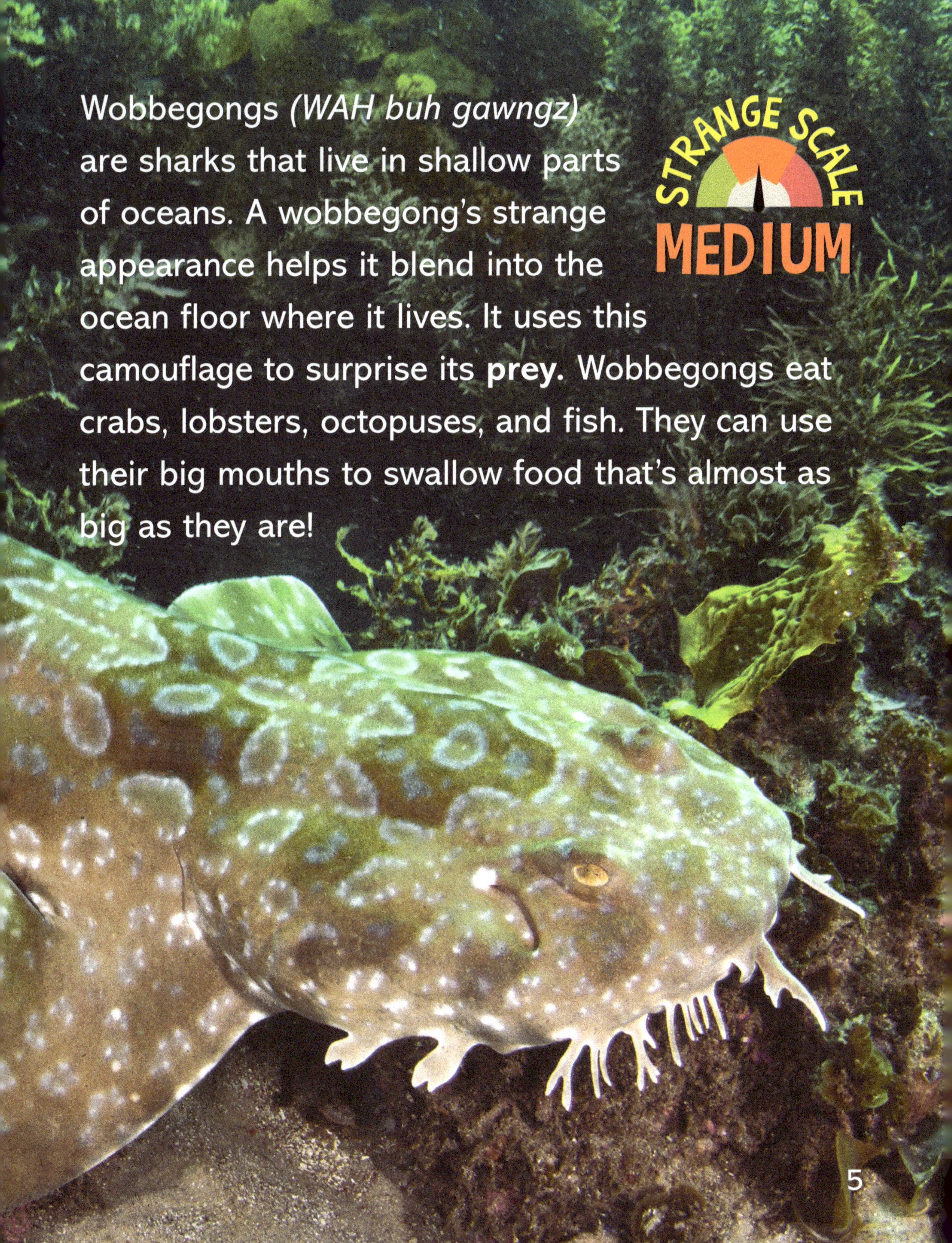

Wobbegongs *(WAH buh gawngz)* are sharks that live in shallow parts of oceans. A wobbegong's strange appearance helps it blend into the ocean floor where it lives. It uses this camouflage to surprise its **prey.** Wobbegongs eat crabs, lobsters, octopuses, and fish. They can use their big mouths to swallow food that's almost as big as they are!

TREE KANGAROO

Tree kangaroos look much different than their kangaroo cousins. Kangaroos grow to be almost three times the size of tree kangaroos!

These small animals are a type of marsupial. Marsupials are mammals whose babies are born very small and continue to grow in a special pouch on the mother's stomach. Tree kangaroos are closely related to kangaroos. But they are smaller and fuzzier. Like their name says, tree kangaroos live mostly in trees.

TAPIR

A tapir *(TAY puhr)* looks like a pig. But it's actually more closely related to horses and rhinoceroses. Tapirs have short, heavy bodies and thick necks. A tapir has a short, stubby trunk for a nose.

SEA BUTTERFLY

Sea butterflies are snails with see-through shells that live in the ocean. Sea butterflies get their name from a pair of fleshy, wing-like structures that they flap like the wings of a butterfly. This movement helps sea butterflies swim through the open water. Sea butterflies are small and fragile. Most measure less than 2/5 inch (1 centimeter) long.

Some sea butterflies carry a heavy shell. This shell can make them sink if they stop moving. To stop sinking, these sea butterflies make a large parachute out of **mucus,** which keeps them afloat! **(Mucus** is that slimy goo that stuffs up your nose sometimes.)

SAIGA

The saiga *(SY guh)* is a strange-looking mammal that owes its strangeness to its large, flexible nose. It uses its nose to keep out of its lungs the dust stirred up by the saiga as they move about in large **herds.** In winter, the nose warms up cold air before it enters the lungs.

PORTUGUESE MAN-OF-WAR

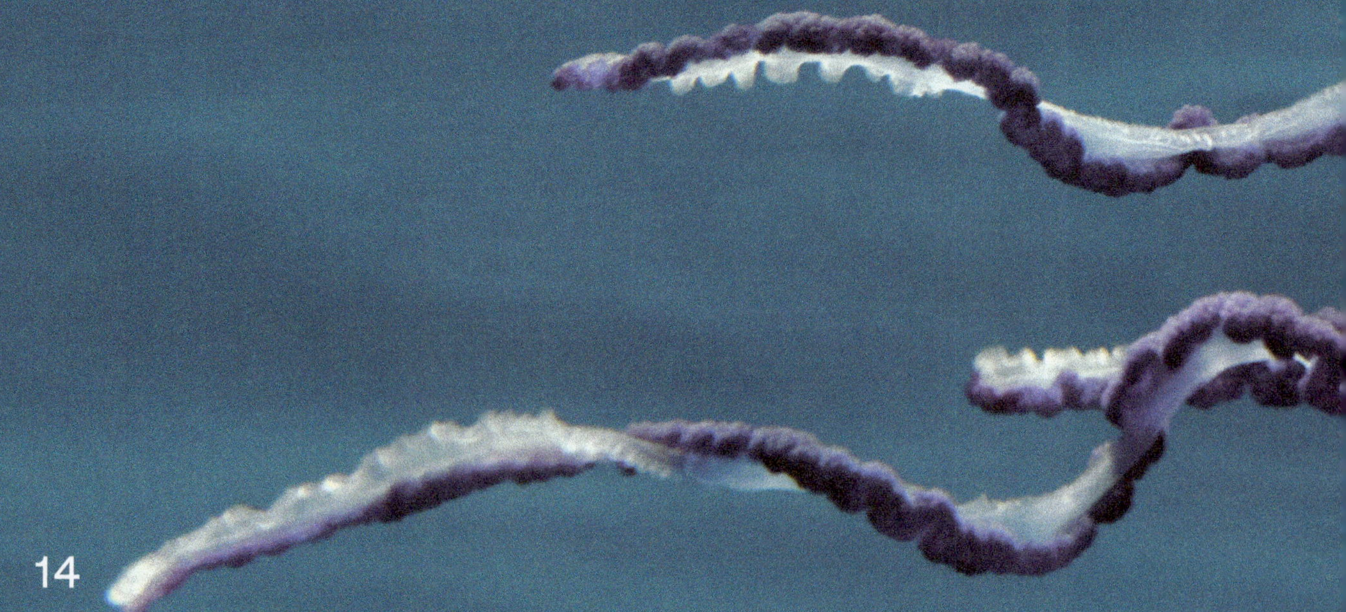

This sea creature looks like a jellyfish. But it's not just a single animal. The Portuguese man-of-war is actually a colony of special animals. The smaller animals that make up the Portuguese man-of-war can't survive on their own, so they work together and live like one larger animal.

AYE-AYE

The aye-aye is a small **primate.**
Primates are a group of animals
that includes human beings and
monkeys. The aye-aye has funny-
looking front teeth that always
grow. Aye-ayes have long, skinny fingers. Their
middle finger on each hand is especially long.

Aye-ayes hunt for insects by tapping on tree branches. Their extra-long fingers let them tap very quickly—up to 8 times every second! They listen for echoes to choose where to chew into the branch.

OSTRACOD

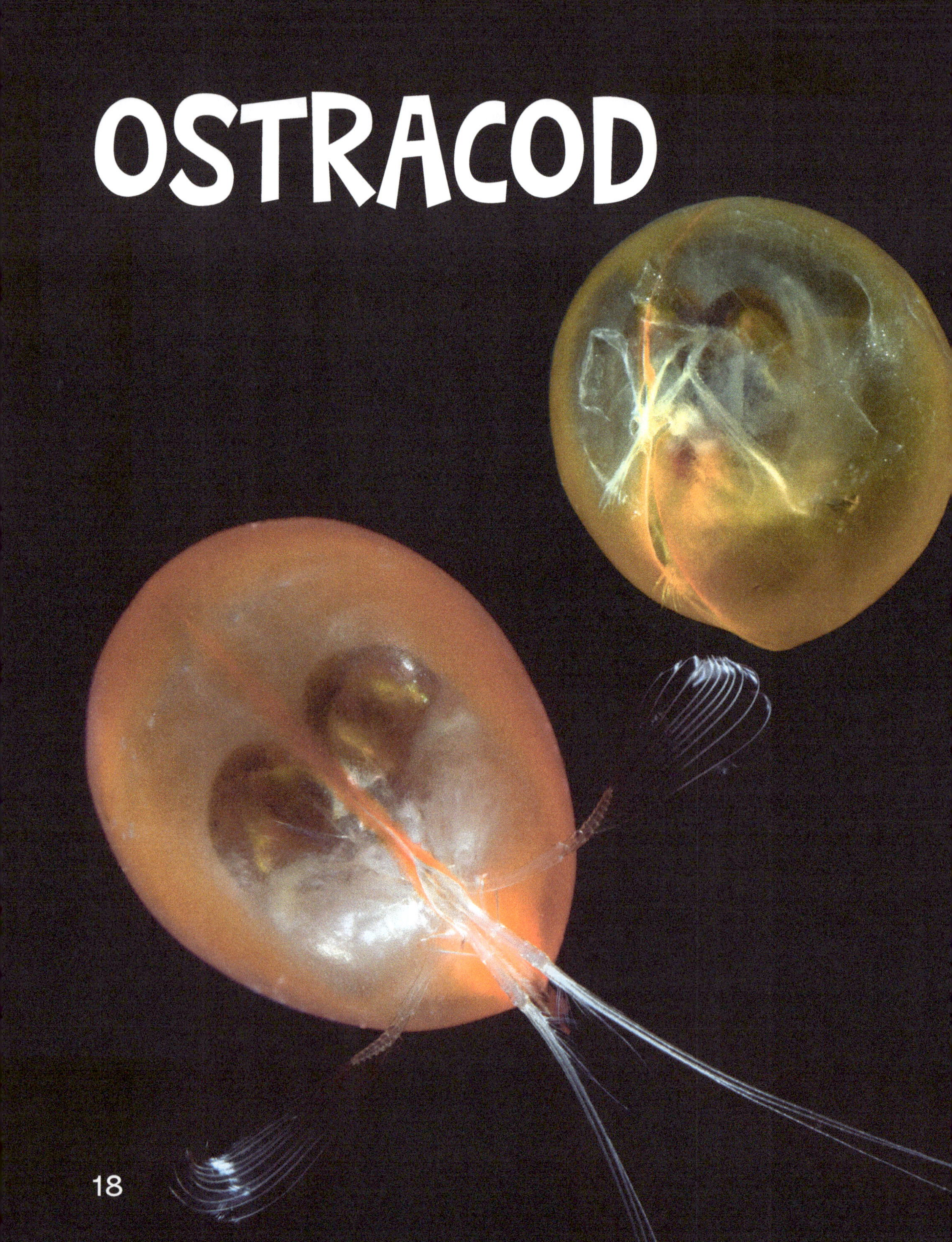

Ostracods are relatives of crabs
and shrimp. The largest ones have
bright orange-red bodies about
the size and shape of cherries!
These ostracods live deep in the
ocean where very little light reaches. In the
black deep-sea waters, they blend almost
completely into the darkness.

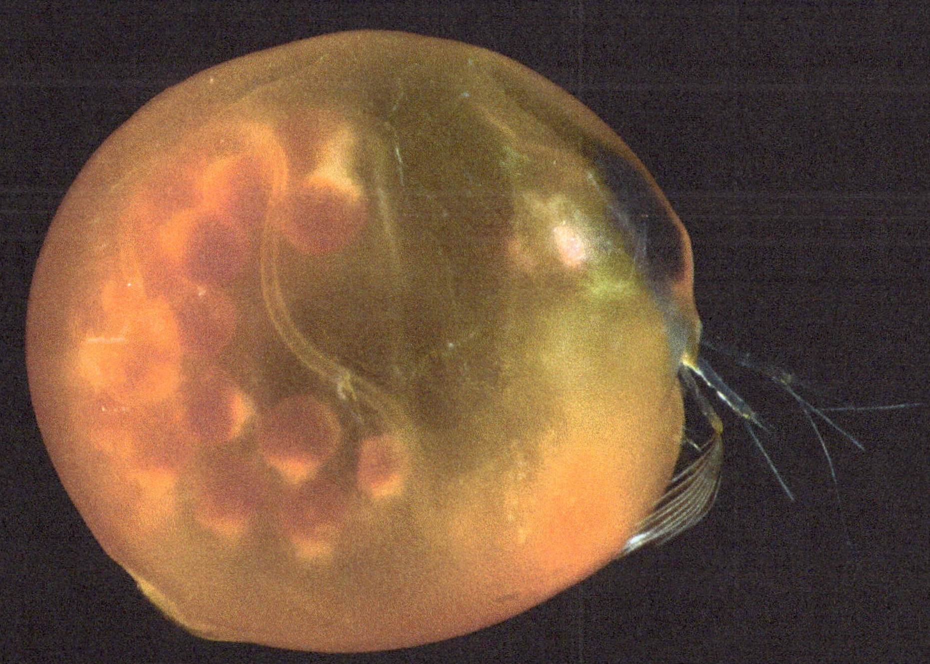

19

ACORN WORM

Acorn worms are strange ocean animals. Some burrow in the sand on the ocean floor, like earthworms, and can grow to be more than 5 feet long! Others swim or float in the ocean current.

The acorn worm in the picture has a funny scientific name. It's called *Yoda purpurata*, which means "purple Yoda." It's named after Yoda from the *Star Wars*™ movies!

Strange Creatures of the Deep

The oceans are filled with crazy-looking creatures. Scientists find new ocean-dwelling animals all the time! Here are some of the strangest among them.

Stargazer fish

Flower hat jelly

Binocular fish

Psychedelic frogfish

Tasseled scorpionfish

OLM

Olms are mostly blind. They have very small, simple eyes that are covered by a layer of skin. Their eyes can still tell light from dark, and olms swim away from the light. Olms find their way through the water by using their other senses.

The olm is a type of salamander.
Salamanders are harmless animals
that look like lizards but are
amphibians. Olms spend almost all
of their lives underwater. They live
in the cold, dark waters of caves.

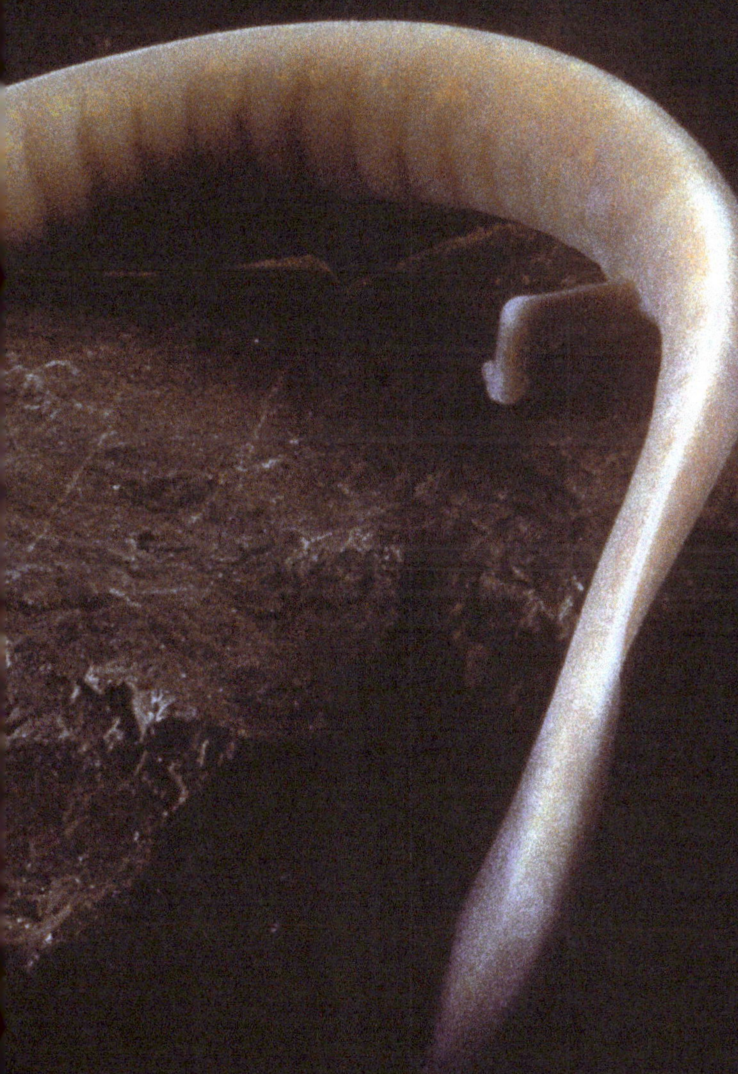

OKAPI

Okapis are only about 5 feet (1.5 meters) tall. Giraffes are 9 feet (2.7 meters) tall at their shoulder, and their long necks make them much taller!

The okapi *(oh KAH pee)* is a **rare** animal that lives in the forests of central Africa. The okapi is related to giraffes. But with its shorter neck and striped legs, the okapi looks more like a zebra!

NUDIBRANCH

Nudibranchs *(NOO duh brangks)* live in the ocean. They are a type of mollusk *(MOL uhsk),* a group of soft-bodied animals that have no bones. Snails, slugs, clams, oysters, squids, and octopuses are all mollusks. Most mollusks have a hard outer shell to protect their soft body. Nudibranchs shed their shells early in life. They come in crazy shapes and lots of bright colors!

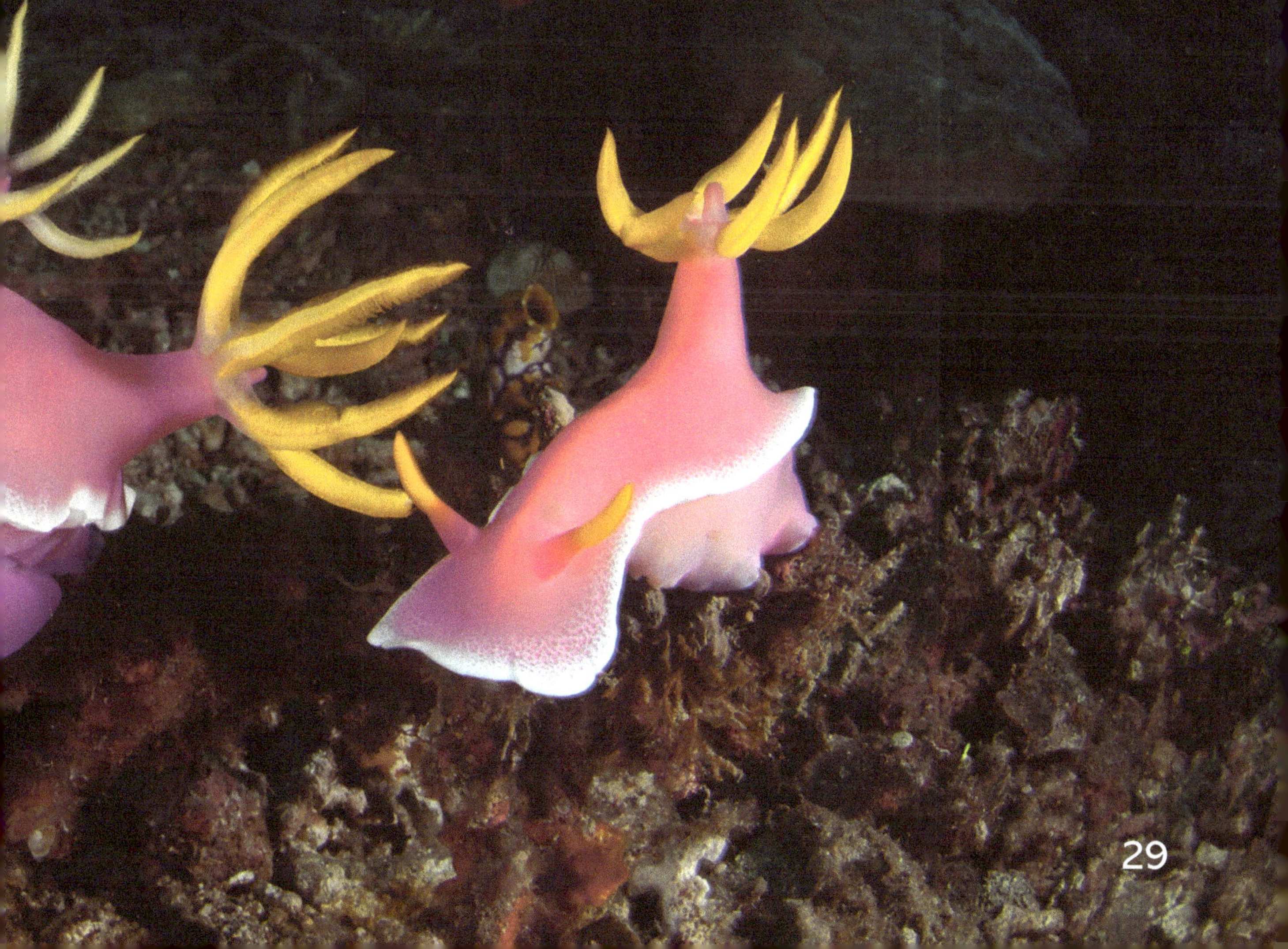

Colorful Creatures

There are lots of animals with strange and unexpected colors. Some use their flashy colors to blend into their surroundings. Others might use them to keep **predators** away. Check out some of the most colorful creatures!

Green lynx spider

Blue lobster

Pink katydid
Blue-footed booby
Red slug

AGOUTI

Agoutis *(uh GOO teez)* are a type of rodent.
Such animals as squirrels and mice are also
rodents. Agoutis have small rounded ears,
long legs, and either a very short tail or
no tail at all. They look a bit like squirrels
without tails, but agoutis grow to the size
of house cats!

GARDEN EELS

34

These fish look like plants growing in a garden! Garden eels live in warm parts of oceans. They bury themselves in the sand of the sea floor and poke their heads out. Garden eels usually live in large groups.

BINTURONG

The binturong *(BIHN tyuh rong)* is sometimes called the bearcat. But it is not closely related to bears or cats. The binturong lives in trees and belongs to a group of animals called civets *(SIHV ihtz)*. It has thick, shaggy hair and black tufted ears with white tips. It sleeps during the day and moves about at night.

The binturong can grip things with the tip of its large, muscular tail.

FROGFISH

Frogfish are fish with wide, froglike mouths and broad, leglike fins. Frogfish use bright colors and patterns to blend into their surroundings. When **prey** comes near, they pounce!

COLUGO

Colugos *(kuh LOO gohz)*, sometimes called flying lemurs, are mammals that live in trees. Colugos are about the size of house cats. They can glide as far as 100 yards (90 meters) from tree to tree. But they don't actually fly. Colugos have large folds of skin between their front and back legs that they use to glide.

Whoa!

When colugos spread their legs, their flaps of skin form "wings." They are sometimes called flying lemurs because they can glide through the air!

GIRAFFE-NECKED WEEVIL

Weevils are beetles with a long
snout. They are pests that attack
crops on farms. The giraffe weevil
is named for its long neck!

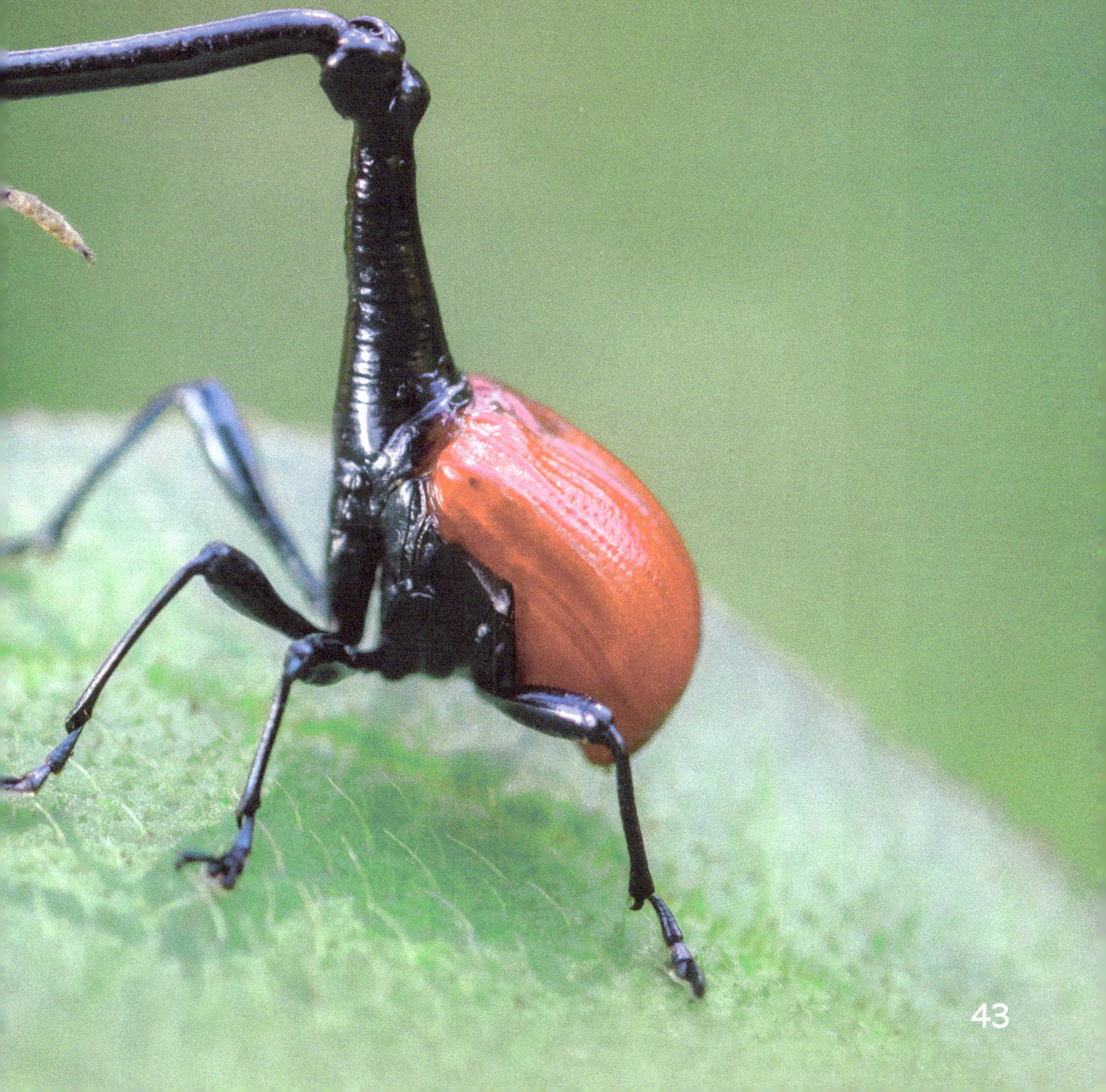

Creepy Crawlies

There are insects of all shapes, colors, and sizes. Some bugs grow to be huge. Yuck! Take a look at some strange and creepy big bugs.

Puss moth caterpillar

Giant prickly stick insect

Giant weta

Goliath beetle
Orb-weaver
spider

Glossary

Herd
a group of animals of one kind living together.

Mucus
a slimy liquid that is produced in parts of animals' bodies.

Predator
an animal that hunts, kills, and eats other animals.

Prey
an animal that is hunted, killed, and eaten by another; to hunt, kill, and eat another animal.

Primate
a member of the highest group of mammals, which includes human beings, apes, and monkeys.

Rare
not often seen or found.

Index

Acknowledgments

Cover: © Wild Wonders of Europe/Hodalic/Nature Picture Library;
© Jurgen Freund, Nature Picture Library

4-5 © Alex Mustard, Nature Picture Library

6-7 © Dave Watts, Nature Picture Library

8-9 © Edwin Giesbers, Nature Picture Library

10-11 © Solvin Zankl, Nature Picture Library

12-13 © Igor Shpilenok, Nature Picture Library

14-15 © Wild Wonders of Europe/Lundgren/Nature Picture Library

16-17 © Nick Garbutt, Nature Picture Library; © Mark Carwardine, Nature Picture Library

18-19 © David Shale, Nature Picture Library

20-21 © David Shale, Nature Picture Library; © Dan Jamieson, Shutterstock

22-23 © Pete Oxford, Nature Picture Library; © Doug Perrine, Nature Picture Library; © Alex Mustard, Nature Picture Library; © Minden Pictures/SuperStock; © Solvin Zankl, Nature Picture Library; © David Shale, Nature Picture Library

24-25 © Wild Wonders of Europe/Hodalic/Nature Picture Library

26-27 © Aflo/Nature Picture Library

28-29 © Jurgen Freund, Nature Picture Library

30-31 © Pete Oxford, Nature Picture Library; © John Cancalosi, Nature Picture Library; © Sue Daly, Nature Picture Library; © Robert Pickett, Visuals Unlimited/Nature Picture Library; © Fabrice Cahez, Nature Picture Library

32-33 © Claudio Contreras, Nature Picture Library

34-35 © Jurgen Freund, Nature Picture Library; © Alex Mustard, Nature Picture Library

36-37 © Edwin Giesbers, Nature Picture Library

38-39 © Alex Mustard, Nature Picture Library

40-41 © Tony Heald, Nature Picture Library

42-43 © Alex Hyde, Nature Picture Library

44-45 © Piotr Naskrecki, Minden Pictures/SuperStock; © Ingo Arndt, Nature Picture Library; © Mark Carwardine, Nature Picture Library; © John Abbott, Nature Picture Library; © Koragit/Shutterstock